T0020154

TABLE OF CONTENTS

REVOLUTION BEGINS

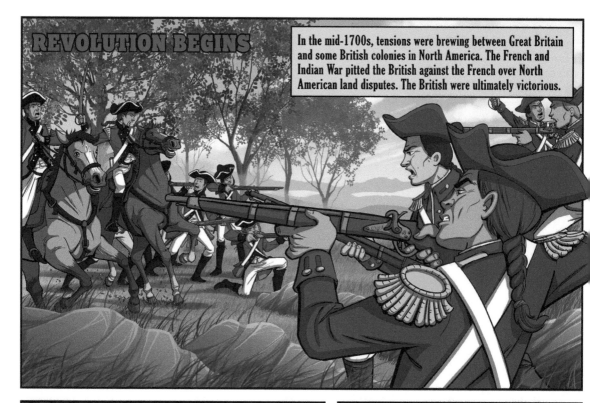

In the mid-1700s, tensions were brewing between Great Britain and some British colonies in North America. The French and Indian War pitted the British against the French over North American land disputes. The British were ultimately victorious.

After the war, Britain needed to pay off its war debts. Since much of their war against the French was fought in North America, the British felt the colonists should help pay.

The British Parliament began passing laws that imposed taxes on the colonists. The colonies had no direct representation in Parliament, so they had no say in these laws.

No taxation without representation!

No taxation without representation!

The Stamp Act of 1765 forced colonists to buy expensive stamps for all printed documents. In the 1760s, a group called the Sons of Liberty formed to resist the Stamp Act.

In 1773, angered by the terms of a new tax on tea, the Sons of Liberty destroyed a shipment of tea in Boston Harbor. The British responded by closing Boston's harbor and taking away the Massachusetts colony's right to self-govern.

This angered many colonists. They formed their own governing body, the Continental Congress. They also began forming militia groups made up of local citizens.

In April 1775, British troops marched toward Concord, Massachusetts, to seize colonial weapons and round up some patriot leaders. But the colonial militia intercepted them at Lexington. A shot was fired, and a battle ensued. The Battle of Lexington began the American Revolution.

On July 2, 1776, the Continental Congress voted in favor of independence from Great Britain. Two days later, it was made official with the proclamation of the Declaration of Independence.

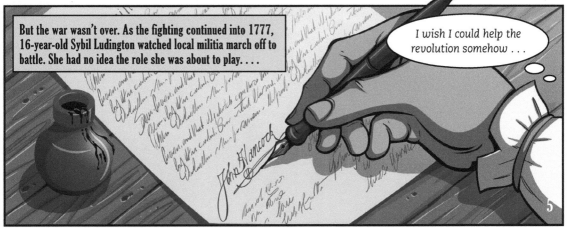

But the war wasn't over. As the fighting continued into 1777, 16-year-old Sybil Ludington watched local militia march off to battle. She had no idea the role she was about to play. . . .

I wish I could help the revolution somehow . . .

Sybil Ludington was born in what was then Fredericksburg, New York. Her father, Henry, made a living as a farmer and mill owner. When he was in his late teens, Henry enlisted to fight in the French and Indian War.

Papa! Tell the story about the Battle of Quebec!

It was September 1759. The last important battle of the war . . .

In the middle of the night, we sailed up the Saint Lawrence River and landed quietly near Quebec City. Then, a group of us scaled a cliff and captured a French outpost. By dawn, more than 4,000 of us stretched across the Plains of Abraham.

During the Revolutionary War, Colonel Ludington became an aide to George Washington. He was in command of a group of local militia.

The militia trained in the yard of the Ludington farm. Colonel Ludington often had to leave home to lead his men in battle.

As the eldest, you have many responsibilities while I'm gone, Sybil. Help your mother. And watch over your siblings.

I will, Father.

And remember, outlaws have been known to roam the area. They'll steal whatever they can. Protect the family if need be.

C-A-T spells cat?

That's right.

I wish I was out there, under the sun, riding my horse.

Come on, Star. Let's go for a ride!

THU-THUMP! THU-THUMP!

THWACK!

POW!

Got it!

With Papa gone, I need to make sure I can protect the family.

It's not very ladylike to shoot guns!

On April 26, 1777, the Ludington family was at home when a sound startled them.

11

What brings you here? Who are you?

A messenger . . . Colonel, the British . . . Danbury . . . !

Sybil! Fetch him some water!

Thousands of British soldiers are raiding Danbury!

Danbury? That's where the militia's weapons are stored!

They are setting fire to homes and buildings. . . .

. . . seizing as many weapons as they can . . .

... and destroying the rest!

I need to gather my men. Tonight! We must set off for Danbury and intercept the British.

But the militiamen are all at home! Spread out over 40 miles. Who will call them to duty?

We must stop the British before they can do any more damage!

I will.

Sybil, no! It's late and dark outside! It's far too dangerous. What about the outlaws roaming the woods?

I'll be careful, Mother.

Henry, please. Might you go instead?

I must stay here to command my men when they arrive.

I can try to continue on. I . . . I just need a bit of rest.

He's much too tired. And he doesn't know this area like I do.

You'd have to cover 40 miles . . .

A REVOLUTIONARY RIDE

Sybil set off on the road to Lake Carmel in the thick darkness of night.

It's so dark in the woods. But I'm not scared. I have a mission to accomplish!

There it is, Star! The Brown home. Our first stop . . . with many more to come!

Who's there?

BANG!

BANG!

Mr. Brown, the British are burning Danbury! Grab your weapons. Muster at Colonel Ludington's at daybreak!

Sybil Ludington! What—?

And spread the word!

17

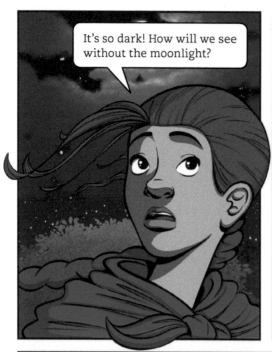

It's so dark! How will we see without the moonlight?

You're right. I don't need the moon when I have you, Star. Onward to Carmel!

Sybil rode three more miles to the town of Carmel, New York.

The British are burning Danbury! Muster at Ludington's at daybreak!

Who is the messenger?

It's a girl!

Within an hour of Sybil's departure, militia began arriving at the Ludingtons' farm. Colonel Ludington prepared the men for the 17-mile march to Danbury.

A young messenger girl told me to come here!

Over there. The militia is preparing to march to Danbury!

Mahopac Pond! I need to stay alert. This is a favorite spot for outlaws to hide and steal from passersby.

Whoa! Did you hear something too, Star?

CLANG!

CLANG!

Sybil continued riding, delivering her message from house to house and town to town. Sometimes the path was so narrow she had to dismount and walk.

We have to keep moving, Star.

Drat! So muddy!

SQUISH!

It's so dark and cold. But I must forge ahead! I must alert the rest of the men.

At least I'm not alone.

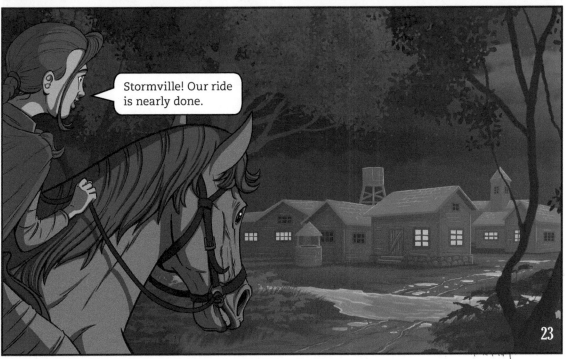

Stormville! Our ride is nearly done.

23

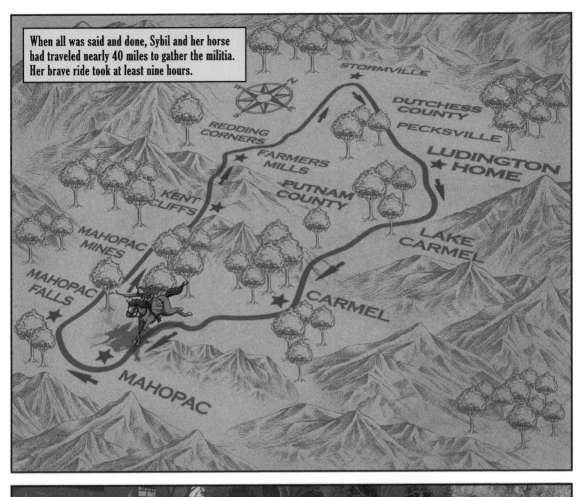

When all was said and done, Sybil and her horse had traveled nearly 40 miles to gather the militia. Her brave ride took at least nine hours.

STORMVILLE

DUTCHESS COUNTY

PECKSVILLE

REDDING CORNERS

FARMERS MILLS

LUDINGTON HOME

KENT CLIFFS

PUTNAM COUNTY

MAHOPAC MINES

LAKE CARMEL

MAHOPAC FALLS

CARMEL

MAHOPAC

The militia was too late to save Danbury, but they surprised the redcoats as they retreated. Even though they were badly outnumbered, the Americans succeeded in chasing the British from the area.

The British fled to their ships in Westport, Connecticut. They never again attempted an inland raid in the area.

27

SYBIL LUDINGTON RIDES ON

The American Revolution continued for many years following Sybil Ludington's midnight ride. In the summer of 1777, the Americans were beginning to lose hope. Then in October 1777, an American victory at the Battle of Saratoga in New York reignited Americans' hopes of winning the war.

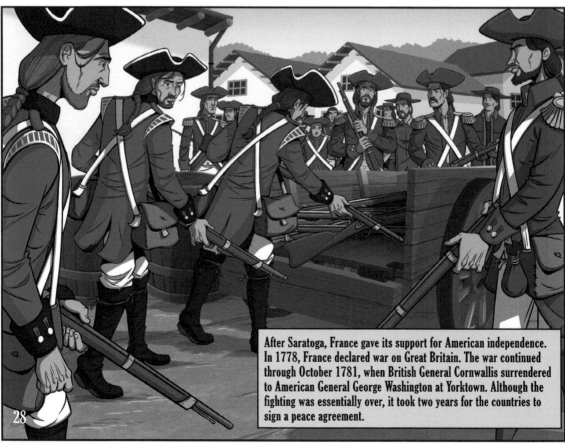

After Saratoga, France gave its support for American independence. In 1778, France declared war on Great Britain. The war continued through October 1781, when British General Cornwallis surrendered to American General George Washington at Yorktown. Although the fighting was essentially over, it took two years for the countries to sign a peace agreement.

Sybil Ludington married Edmond Ogden in 1784. The couple had a son, Henry, who was named after Sybil's father. Sybil lived a long life and died in 1839 at the age of 77.

Sadly, Sybil Ludington was not recognized as a hero in her lifetime. In fact, her ride was nearly forgotten until 1907, when a biography of her father, Colonel Henry Ludington, was published. The book told the story of Sybil's ride, capturing the interest of many.

Historical markers were later placed along Sybil Ludington's possible route. In 1961, a bronze statue of Sybil, created by sculptor Anna Hyatt Huntington, was dedicated. The statue stands along Sybil's route, near Lake Gleneida in Carmel Hamlet, New York. It honors the great heroism of a young 16-year-old girl and the dangerous feat she undertook for freedom.

GLOSSARY

colonies (KAH-luh-neez)—the 13 groups of people living in North America before the Revolutionary War; they were ruled by Great Britain.

Continental Congress (kahn-tuh-nen-tuhl KAHNG-gruhs)—leaders from the 13 original American colonies who made up the American government from 1774 to 1789

forge (fohrj)—to move forward slowly but steadily

intercepted (in-tur-SEP-tid)—taken, seized, or stopped before reaching an intended destination

militia (muh-LISH-uh)—a group of volunteer citizens who serve as soldiers in emergencies

outlaw (OUT-law)—a person who has broken the law and is hiding or fleeing to avoid punishment

Parliament (PAR-luh-muhnt)—the national legislature of Great Britain

revolution (rev-uh-LOO-shuhn)—an uprising by a group of people against a system of government or a way of life

seize (SEEZ)—to take something by force

troops (TROOPS)—a group of soldiers

READ MORE

Abbott, E.F. *Sybil Ludington: Revolutionary War Rider*. New York: Macmillan, 2016.

Amstel, Marsha. Adapted by Amanda Doering Tourville. *The Horse-Riding Adventure of Sybil Ludington, Revolutionary War Messenger*. Minneapolis: Graphic Universe, 2013.

Marsico, Katie. *Sybil Ludington's Revolutionary War Story*. Minneapolis: Lerner Publications, 2018.

INTERNET SITES

National Women's History Museum—Sybil Ludington
https://www.womenshistory.org/education-resources/biographies/sybil-ludington

Sybil Ludington, the Teen Patriot Who Outrode Paul Revere
https://www.kidsdiscover.com/quick-reads/sybil-ludington-teen-patriot-outrode-paul-revere/

American History for Kids—Sybil Ludington
https://www.americanhistoryforkids.com/sybil-ludington/

INDEX